30985

798 23

D0364608

LONDON BOROUGH OF GREENWICH

GREENWICH LIBRARIES

RESERVE STOCK (P)

LSZ0016

GREENWICH LIBRARIES

3 8028 00858807 8

Riding
Dialogue

RIDING
DIALOGUE

written and illustrated by
Peter Churchill

BLANDFORD PRESS   LONDON

First published 1973
by Blandford Press Ltd
167 High Holborn, London WC1V6PH
© *Blandford Press Ltd 1973*

ISBN ◖ 7137 0614 7

All rights reserved. No part of this book may be reproduced or transmitted in
any form or by any means, electronic or mechanical, including photocopying,
recording or by any information storage and retrieval system, without per-
mission in writing from the publisher.

Text set in 11 on 13 Times New Roman
and printed in Great Britain by
Unwin Brothers Limited
The Gresham Press
Old Woking Surrey
A member of the Staples Printing Group

30985

798 23

Contents

The only Golden Rule is
that there are no Golden Rules.

George Bernard Shaw

Acknowledgments

My personal thanks to Madame Simone Lemaigre-Dubreuil for her kindness, generosity and forbearance in allowing me to use the horses and facilities of her lovely estate near Fontainebleau for some of the photography. Further, to Richard Reincke, my photographer, thanks for his patience and understanding.

P.C.

The following are thanked for their kind permission to reproduce the photographs on the pages indicated:

German Embassy *73, 81*
Novosti Press Agency *85* (both pictures), *86*
Sport and General Press Agency *72, 75, 76*
United States Travel Service *82*
Whitbread and Co Ltd *74, 77*

O.K., so we're not talking.

8

1 The beginning of the dialogue

In my first book, *Riding for Everbody*, I tried to create and explain a
simple A B C of riding for the absolute beginner. In the second,
Progressive Steps in Riding, the object was to define further the basic
principles of riding and training. *Riding Dialogue* will follow the theme
and, I hope, the simplicity set by the other two, but will attempt to
explain, perhaps for the first time, the 'language' of the horse: the
signs, and possible objections, of the horse whilst in training. It will
explain the problems that will arise when one begins advanced riding
and competing—the 'riding conversation' between horse and rider.

I often find that the amateur rider finds it difficult to know when
the horse is objecting and when it is uncomfortable or just not capable.
When I say 'amateur' I mean those who ride to enjoy the sport
and its techniques. If the rider is to improve, and if the horse is to
improve, then the situation must be 'read' accurately.

Riding is a sport. We do it because we like it, because we want to
be good at it, and we like to win. Unlike many other sports it involves
two living elements—horse and man—both of which must be trained
and have aptitude and ability. I am not attempting to talk about
Olympic equitation: this is for a chosen few. I am concerned with the
majority who ride for enjoyment, appreciate the art, and wish to
perform to the best of the ability both of themselves and of the horse:
those, for example, who are trying to do something in the field of
competition for their enjoyment and fun. This is likely to be in the
smaller show-jumping competitions, one- and two-day events, and
riding and Pony Club dressage tests.

It is very easy to turn any subject into a complicated science, especially in book form, and it is equally easy to 'waffle on' about what can happen and what can be done about it. It is more difficult to simplify techniques and problems, but this is essential in riding. First, because we are dealing with an animal of simple intelligence; second, because we are dealing with an animal that is naturally timid, easily frightened, and easily confused; and third, because two mentalities—human and animal—are attempting to work together, and nothing can run riot more quickly than these two if allowed to become complicated!

It is not possible in the compass of a small book, in my opinion, to give general solutions to problems. (So often I have seen this bring disastrous results for the reader and his horse or pony.) There is no magic formula—no secret recipe. There are so many personal aspects and unknown quantities involved that a generalisation of the solutions can only lead to more confusion. Where the author can help his reader is in putting before him the situations that are likely to arise and suggest a way of analysing them, based on his own experience; in my case, based on several years of training, racing, show-jumping and eventing, and almost as many years in making a fool of myself! This happens to us all and nothing can make you feel smaller than your beautifully turned out, beautifully trained horse suddenly deciding to do something quite the opposite of what you had intended! That's the fun and fascination of the sport, because when things go right it is one of the most marvellous experiences one can have. So don't be afraid of things going wrong. Relax and enjoy yourself and you will find that your horse will do the same.

I will never forget a story of a racehorse trainer friend of mine. He was one of the all-time greats as a steeplechase-jockey, and later established himself as a top-class trainer. I used to ride the odd (sometimes they were really ODD!) two-year-old for him on the flat. He had a great influence on my riding life, but unfortunately has now departed from us.

Bill, let us call him, had been sent a two-year-old by a very well-known owner. The two-year-old arrived the day before he was due to run in his first race. Because of this Bill and I did not get much time to study him or to try him. The following day we were in the paddock, the runners parading before the public. The owner, who had flown over for the race, was explaining to Bill the breeding of the two-year-old—

the number of winners the dam had produced, the great winners the grand-dam had produced, the classic winners the sire had produced, his illustrious brothers and half-brothers, etc. etc. He then turned to dear old Bill and asked his opinion. 'Sir,' Bill replied, 'has all this been explained to the little horse?'

The anecdote contains a relevant and important point; we should not further discuss the conversation between man and beast without first considering the factors that help in deciding that the beast and the man are the right ones for the job.

With the horse it is fairly easy, but with the rider we can only put forward theories. In *Progressive Steps in Riding* I went into some detail on the importance of the shape and mental attitude of the rider. At that time I said, 'No matter how you are made, you can learn to ride and enjoy the sport of riding horses.' I feel, however, that many people go through stages of frustration whilst learning, simply because it has not been explained to them that their shape is important to their rate of progress. When they know what rate of progress they can expect from themselves, they settle down to steady improvement and begin to enjoy it.' So rather like Bill's two-year-old, if you go to scale at 180 lbs, the fact that your father was a great flat-race jockey is not going to make you a Lester Piggott! Equally who is to say you may not be a good polo-player, or show-jumping rider, or riding club dressage champion. Later we shall discuss the 'secret conversation' between horse and rider, but perhaps the first, most important step is the secret (and honest) dialogue between you and yourself. Decide which of the equestrian sports (or perhaps simply the pastime of riding as often as possible) you think you are suited for and then make sure you know as much as you can about it. Only you can decide this. No book, nor horse, nor magic formula can do it for you.

The horse for the job

With the horse, known facts and practices can be put into operation and make the decision for us. For example, you may wonder why your riding club horse is always nearer the last three than the first three in the club's one-day event. Yet he seems to do everything reasonably well—as well as he can. He jumps all the cross-country

11

fences; he never refuses anything in the show-jumping; he performs all the movements in the dressage test. He does not show any objections, yet he cannot get into the winners' enclosure. He is in a way conversing with you if you can hear it. He could be saying, 'Look, mate, you're a nice guy. I'm doing my best, but this isn't my game, you know!' One can know all the steps of the tango, and still be a rotten dancer.

Let's theorise further, let's imagine this horse. He is probably a stocky, well-built animal, with a short neck, very powerful hindquarters, plenty of bone, legs rather thick and with a high leg action in front. Not an ugly horse but at the same time not the sort you would see in the paddock at Longchamp. He is most probably a very generous creature and the type that puts a lot of leg action into covering a short distance of ground. In other words not the type that would object to anything in particular but by the sheer mechanics of his conformation is not made for galloping fast in long, wide open, cross-country events. He is the sort that would possibly adapt himself to the more restrictive area of the show-jumping ring; his short strides fitting him well for the shorter distances between the jumps; his powerful hind-quarters giving him 'lift' over the more uniform fences. This type of horse often makes a very useful and consistent club show-jumper.

The object of this little exercise, which as you can see is purely hypothetical, is to put before you in the simplest possible terms an illustration of how to consider the horse in relation to the job he is going to do.

At first this can only be based on the conformation and the action of the horse. Later we will be able to make assessments based on the mental aptitude and attitude of the animal as well as his physique.

Considering the conformation of the horse

The inter-action of the various parts of the horse *vis-à-vis* his disposition and fluency are of paramount importance to his efficiency and performance. It is no good asking a horse with too straight a shoulder to come downhill fast. The upright angle of his shoulder blade will restrict the pendulum movement of the joint and minimise the length of his stride. Equally a horse that is too long in his body will not be able to 'quicken' himself (accelerate) over a short distance. Again a horse

Shoulder too straight.

Good shoulder.

that is too short in the neck will have problems in balancing himself, as the neck is the horse's natural balancing pole. Further he will tend to be an uncomfortable ride for a tall man. The shortness of his neck will give the rider the unnerving illusion of sitting on the horse's head, especially when riding across country; the horse for the job and the man for the job, remember? The horse with too long a neck will have the opposite effect: that of forcing the rider too far back. This type also tends to be weak in his neck muscles, thus, once again, making balance difficult.

These lengths and dimensions must be in relation to the whole. A horse that has a body which is out of proportion to his neck, or his

Pastern too upright (shortens action).   Pastern with good slope.

legs, or his hindquarters etc., is not going to be an easy horse to train or ride.

There are always, of course, exceptions to the rule. There have been and always will be animals whose conformation leaves much to be desired but which have proved to be absolute world-beaters, just as there are film and television stars who are far from being glamour boys! Why or how this happens I don't think anybody can explain; a certain magic, perhaps? All I can tell you is that among the finest-made horses in Europe, I have ridden some that have proved to be utterly useless; I have also ridden some of the worst-made animals, and these have almost invariably proved to be worse than useless.

A good example of this was a crack young hurdler that I used to ride out. He was perhaps the best that had been seen for many years; he won the champion hurdle more than once; he was voted Racehorse of the Year and won practically all the valuable races open to a young jumper. Here was a truly great racehorse, but he had far from perfect action and conformation. What he did have was the most perfect pair of shoulders one could wish to see. But to ride? He could hardly trot properly, and his canter had to be seen to be believed! He was not a difficult horse to ride as far as temperament was concerned, in fact he had the natural manners of a gentleman, but to ride at his slower paces he was the most uncomfortable horse I have ever sat on. As his record proved, when on the racecourse and down to the work he loved, those wonderful shoulders came into operation and his long, ground-devouring gallop broke the hearts of all who opposed him. Here was a case of a horse with a good temperament, tremendous courage and spirit, and these cancelled out any faults he may have had in his conformation. His trainer had 'read' right, he saw the signs, he listened to the dialogue. The horse could not operate effectively in his slow paces. All sorts of ways had to be found and tried to get the horse fit and hard for the racecourse. A certain young trainer in Epsom would be the first to tell you how hard he had to 'listen' to his charge, and of many sleepless nights before he produced a real champion!

Then there is the example of a very well-known two-year-old I rode out at Chantilly in France. This was one of the finest bred and most beautiful looking colts I have ever seen or sat on. In all his paces he was an equine version of a Rolls-Royce; an easy, comfortable ride and an easy horse to train. He, too, went on to prove on the racecourse that he was a champion of champions.

As you can see it is not possible to lay down hard and fast rules; it is dangerous to generalise. Each animal must be judged individually and a careful study must be made of his faults and his good points. Only in this way can we minimise the problems and enjoy ourselves in the process.

We can assume, though, that if the pony or horse is made right he will do his job well, be a good ride, and should not present problems in training. When studying the following pages, I want you to bear in mind this opening discussion and the following points:

(*a*) The make and shape of the horse must be relative to the work he is going to do.
(*b*) The rider must adapt himself to the ability of the horse.
(*c*) There *can* be exceptions to the rule.
(*d*) Keep things simple, avoid confusion and above all concentrate on enjoying yourself.

This last point is in my opinion the key to good riding. If the rider is enjoying himself he will relax. If the rider is relaxed then the horse will relax too.

Remember that the horse by origin was a hunted animal, and, like all hunted creatures, is an inborn worrier. By nature the horse is always on the alert, always listening, always watching what is happening around him, so getting him to relax and to concentrate on what we are asking of him is extremely important both for his efficiency and your enjoyment.

Relax and enjoy yourselves.

2 Asking the right 'questions'

This is not, you will have realised by now, a book simply teaching you to ride. It is more a work to help you to improve your technique and your knowledge with and of the horse, to take you 'behind the scenes'.

We have discussed how the shape of the horse can affect his performance and our choice of what we want to do with him. We are concerned of course throughout with the influences that will change or improve the performance the animal will give. Everything we do in riding, training and management will be relative to what he will be capable of doing.

There are two ways of approaching equitation. One is where the rider dominates the horse, and the second is where the horse is educated to do the job with minimum interference from the rider. There are the hundred per cent physical riders who by sheer strength force the animal to do as they command. This is comparatively easy, as practically all horses are easily frightened. This school of thought sees the 'key' to all problems in more and more complicated equipment; special types of schooling fences designed to put the fear of God into any animal (and man!). One meets these types all over the world and at all levels of riding. Their talent as athletes is indisputable and although their talent for equitation may seem to be very limited, they do sometimes get fantastic results. An interesting thing about this group is that two constant facts always show themselves. First, results they may get but their record (man and beast) is often inconsistent. Second, the end product is ugly and gives the impression that the entire performance is difficult to achieve. (It looks too much like hard work for me!). Furthermore, anybody taking over a horse after this kind of handling will find it the task of many months trying to re-educate and calm the unfortunate animal.

If you think this system suits you, and it is not for me to say it is wrong, go ahead and use it—*it is the simplest*—but it has nothing to do with equitation.

The second approach is to educate the horse to do his job with the minimum interference from you. To train him to perform a given task using his natural ability, flair and power. This is the most difficult, the most heartbreaking, the most demanding and the longest method. Riders all over the world are working in this fashion. Again two constant facts emerge. First, results take longer but when achieved the record remains consistent. Second, the end product is pleasant to watch and gives the impression of the entire performance being as easy and as simple as falling off a log. One could, once more, qualify this by adding that anybody taking on a horse after this kind of handling will get nothing but joy from sitting on his back.

If you think this system suits you, then come along with me—*it is the most difficult*—but it is what equitation is all about.

So what happens when we ask for something and the horse says 'No'; in other words when he objects? Here we will be dealing with that fine line between 'No, I can't' and 'No, I won't'. The difference between these two responses is a very fine line so do be careful.

Is it objection or discomfort? We can define, for the object of this exercise, an objection as 'No, I won't', and a discomfort as 'No, I can't'. The simplest way to illustrate this is to take a theoretical case of a problem which presents itself with almost boring regularity—the horse refusing a fence! Of all the people who ride, whether young or old, ninety-nine per cent want to jump some sort of obstacle. How many times have we arrived at the first fence of our local hunter trials on our impeccably turned out 'pride and joy', only to be dumped the other side of the obstacle by our world-beating jumper whilst he looks on innocently from the approach side of the fence! So let's use this as an example of reading the 'conversation'.

Too many experts say that a horse should not be allowed to refuse a fence—this is, of course, rubbish. A horse will, can, and often does refuse a jump and in many cases it is far better that he uses his brains

'Stoking one up'.

and stops, rather than continue blindly on, finishing up by breaking his neck and yours.

There are four main reasons why a horse refuses.

Reason	Dialogue	Objection/Discomfort
(i) Fence is too big (lack of education)	I can't	Discomfort (ignorance)
(ii) Habitual stopper (previous bad training or just plain cheeky or dishonest.)	I won't (or perhaps could?)	Objection
(iii) Dislikes jumping (lacks courage or athletic ability— *maybe ill*)	I won't and I can't	Objection and discomfort
(iv) Presented badly by the rider	non-existent	Discomfort, most certainly. Objecting, not to the obstacle, but to *you*!

Always take into consideration that the horse may not be well. Check him over for any signs, take his temperature, ensure that he is eating well, etc.

Reason (i) is perhaps one of the most common ones and is usually caused by the rider rushing his horse—asking too much of him too soon—'overfacing' as it is called.

This can be caused when a young horse with a great deal of talent reaches too quickly a standard which is beyond his experience and knowledge but not beyond his capabilities. Finally this situation can be created by the rider presenting the horse badly at the fence, but more of this later.

Imagine you are jumping a young horse at home, at your riding club, or at your riding school. All is going well, you both seem to be enjoying yourselves, and then you arrive at a 'parallel bars'. Suddenly the horse stops—refuses. The first question is, has he 'stopped' or has he 'refused'? There is a subtle but important difference between the two. On the spur of the moment we have to decide which it is. It would be more accurate to substitute, for 'decide', the word 'guess'. How can we then make this guess? You may have noticed that very often a horse 'stops' at a fence for no apparent reason and then just stands there looking at the obstacle. This, for me, is a 'stop', which can be interpreted as 'Sorry, I can't'. The signal that the horse is trying to give is shown by the fact that he remains comparatively calm at the jump. You may also have noticed the horse that will tend to stiffen himself some distance from the fence, skid to a halt in front of it with obvious signs of excitement, looking left and right for a way out and on many occasions half attempt to jump the obstacle thus crashing through it or smashing it to the ground. Here the animal has quite definitely said, 'No, I won't'—this, for me, is a refusal.

As you can see it is possible through a simple reading of the situation to decide very quickly what the horse is trying to say. We have guessed that our imaginary horse has said, 'No, I can't' but we have to make sure. Automatically one turns round and faces the obstacle once more and, let's imagine, once more he stops. If again he has remained fairly calm we can be pretty certain he is saying, 'No, I can't', but if this time he is in more of a panic than the first time we can be fairly certain he is saying, 'No, I won't'.

If this happens in a competition, do not, as one so often sees, attempt to school your horse in public. It may make you feel better but it will not do his future much good. Instead, retire gracefully and go home, and return to the basic schooling in the tranquility of privacy.

Upon getting home let the horse rest up and the following day begin quietly schooling again. Remember first of all to warm him up; limber up his muscles and yours; walking, trotting, cantering, stopping and starting, working on both reins (both directions). Then start jumping him over very small fences and fences that he knows well. Aim all the time to keep the horse calm. Few people will allow a horse to stay calm and yet it is so much better when he is.

Now put up some very low parallel bars. Get off the horse and put the lunge-rein on him. For the best results fit the rein to a lunge cavesson and not to the bridle; also, place a bar at either side of the fence to act as a running rail for the lunge. Then quietly, and at the trot only, work the horse on a circle moving gradually towards the obstacle finally allowing him to go into the fence and pop over it. Do

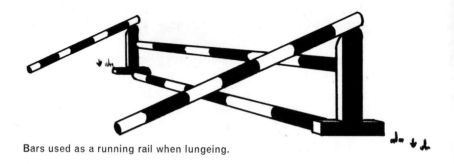

Bars used as a running rail when lungeing.

not forget to lunge the horse in both directions thus encouraging his body to be supple, and don't force him to jump; let him find his own way in. At first, he will jump over the small fence without any problems. Once this is achieved, start to put the bars up one notch at a time. As each jump is successfully completed repeat the process of raising the jump until the height of the previous day is reached. If all has gone well and the horse has shown no signs of objecting, lower the bars again, take the lunge-rein off and get on his back. This time the system will differ slightly in so much as we will now jump the other fences as well as our very low parallel bars. Again as each jump is successful, raise the bars. Remember, once more, keep the horse calm and never force him. Perseverance is always better than force and it will stay in his little head.

If, after all this, it is found that the horse has shown no signs of stopping, we can safely assume that he was saying 'No, I can't', and is now saying, 'Yes, I can'. Now all this is standard stuff which you will find in practically the same form in many riding books. I have repeated it so that I can fix in your mind the system of deciding whether it is 'No, I can't' or 'No, I won't.' In other words, looking at the problem in a simple way, reading the situation correctly, and above all 'listening' to the horse. After all, he's the poor fella who is going to have to do the job in the end, so why not let *him* have some say in the matter.

This form of training takes time and a great deal of patience, but as the horse's confidence and education improves so the problems will diminish. Furthermore you will have more confidence and be proud to have one of the best rides in the country.

If, however, the horse continues to refuse, time after time and day after day, either on the lunge or afterwards when you ride him, then you must study his whole attitude to jumping. For example, should he show signs of trying to avoid you when stopping; of getting overexcited or panicking, or of looking for a way out, then you must assume that he is saying, 'No, I won't'. In this case you are left with one of two choices, (a) to discipline the horse severely and try to force him to jump the fence, (b) to stop jumping him altogether or get rid of him. *I would always advise the latter*. If the horse is jumping because he is frightened of you he will never be consistent. It will always be in the back of his mind and yours, and consequently you will both be seeing problems before they arise or, worse still, when they do not exist! Neither of you will relax, and neither of you will enjoy yourself. For this reason alone it is not what I would call a sport or hobby, more a penance. Some people like that sort of thing! But you, unlike the horse, have a choice.

Here you can see the youngster being left entirely alone to find his own way in and over.

Don't worry about yourself; leave the horse free.

So we now know something of reading, listening to, and understanding the 'conversation' but remember that the dividing line between objection and discomfort is narrow. It is therefore far better if in doubt to try all possible ways to find and analyse the 'discomfort' before deciding that the problem is an 'objection'. Always give the horse the benefit of the doubt.

Is the rider asking the right 'questions'?

This is closely allied to what we have been discussing, so let us return to our table on page 20 and discuss reasons (ii) and (iii). By doing this I will demonstrate to you how we can phrase and re-phrase our 'questions' to the horse. We will start with reason (ii)—the horse that often (as against continually) refuses or stops. This type of animal usually gets himself into a right old sweat whenever something of this nature happens and this is often a sign that he anticipates something dreadful is going to happen. In other words, through previous handling

24

or training he has bad memories of jumping. This can be overcome by posing the 'question' in a different manner. For example, put the fence he does not like in the middle of several very easy fences, making it low and equally easy. Start by jumping the other fences slowly and calmly, each time passing the obstacle he has stopped at. Then gradually as he loosens up pass nearer and nearer to the *béte noire* until eventually, when he is jumping the others, almost nonchalantly have a go at the offending obstacle. If he jumps it first time rub his mane, caress him, reward him. Don't be frightened of being sentimental; there's no law against it, and it is not going to cost you anything. Anyway, there is nobody watching except you and me! When this point is reached, once again, raise the bars little by little. Conversely, should he again stop, go right back to square one jumping the other fences quietly until he is settled and then try the offending one again until he does jump it. If he does—don't forget—be soft.

This is one example of phrasing or rephrasing the questions that we ask of the horse. The basis of the dialogue between man and beast is repetition and illustration, but these techniques will take considerable time, perhaps days, weeks or even months, so the pressure will be on your patience.

Two youngsters working together.

In reason (iii) on p. 20 there are other factors which must be considered. If the rider considers that he has tried all methods of phrasing his 'questions' and has asked them correctly and still he gets no result (answer), then he must accept the possibility that either the horse lacks the courage or the athletic ability for the job, or he just doesn't like jumping. Further, and most important of all, he may be ill. As each problem (objection or discomfort) arises, this is the first check that must be made and the most obvious one. Check next that he is eating properly; check his droppings in the loose-box (for signs of worms, etc.); check his temperature. In other words see that he has no physical excuse and is not feeling off colour.

There is one further aspect relevant to what we have been talking about, and that is the seeing of the 'stride' (reason (iv) in our table.) This is important in view of the points we have just covered, because it is also a way of communicating with the horse, and to be effective it must not be a monologue. What it amounts to in fact is the presenting of the horse to the fence we wish to see the other side of. You see we are forced to use some sort of technique if we wish to leave *terra firma* for a few seconds on the back of a horse, because the horse is not a member of a jumping family, as is the cat or the dog. His body was not created to be as supple as, say, the cat's; he has no nice soft paws to cushion him, nor claws to grab something should disaster strike. Nevertheless we do know that if asked, the horse can jump extremely well, and many seem to enjoy it enormously.

Now what is this 'seeing the stride'? I must have asked a thousand people that question and am still suffering from the stony silence that always followed this sign of my ignorance. To be honest there were many nice people who tried to explain it to me, but I never really understood. Now nearing what I am told is the golden age at which life begins I have at last realised that 'seeing the stride' is not some heavenly vision one sees stretched out before one at the approach to a fence. No, what 'seeing the stride' is all about is rhythm. It is from the horse's rhythm that he gets the impetus to jump the obstacle.

In all sports there are certain things that are difficult to explain, and to these we tend to attach 'labels' or 'terms'. This helps us to describe (or excuse) what we have just done or tried to do without having to go into great detail, when in fact what we are doing is using

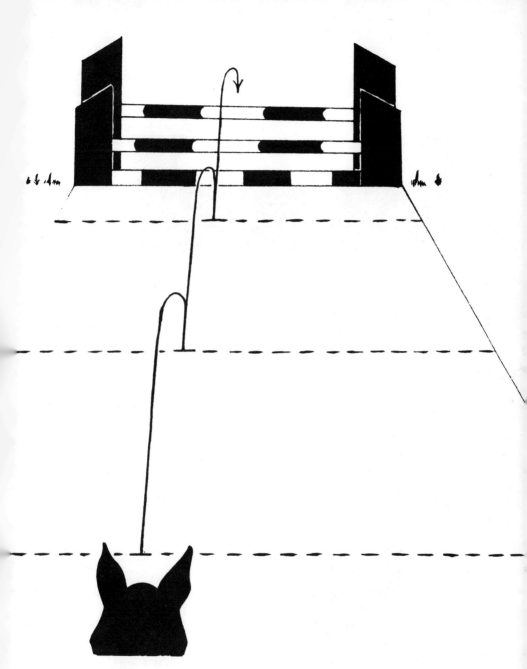

Even stride at spread fence.

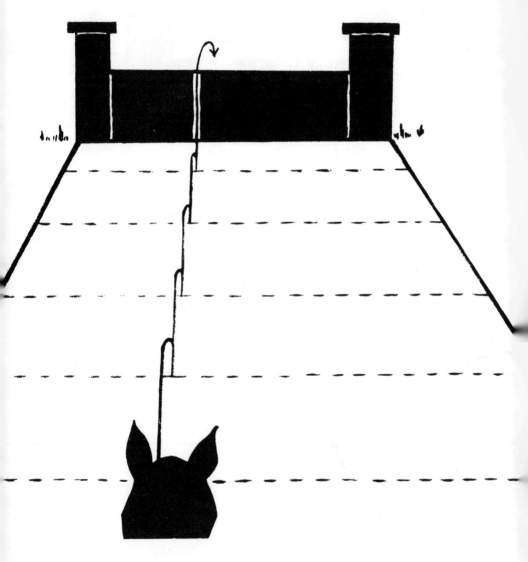

Even stride at upright fence.

a conglomeration of an awful lot of instinct, a great deal of feel and a little bit of technique.

Here again there are two schools of thought. One that says if the horse is held up by physical power such as the strength of the hands or the severity of the equipment put on him until the rider decides the time is right to go or until he 'sees' the right place to take off, and is then ridden with maximum energy, he must jump the fence and clear it.

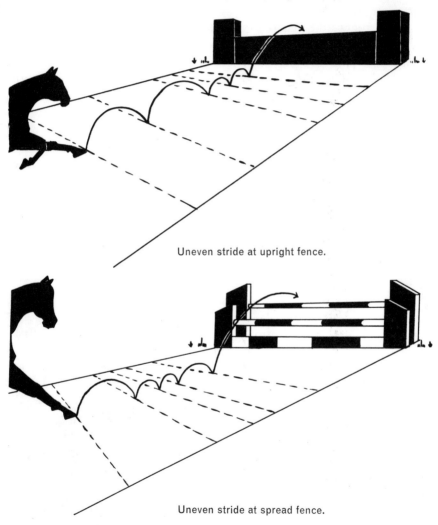

Uneven stride at upright fence.

Uneven stride at spread fence.

Some adherents of this theory believe that the horse can be made to jump higher this way and with greater accuracy. Indeed there are a few riders who are brilliant at this technique.

The other school of thought says that the horse must be taught to jump, to find his own rhythm ('see his own stride'), and decide for himself the point of take-off. The rider also must be taught to feel when the horse has got himself right and then be capable of giving him complete freedom to do the job he has been trained for—jumping the fence. I might add that this requires a cool nerve on the part of the rider and a great deal of self-confidence on the part of the horse. The main difference between these two theories is that the former is a monologue. The rider does all the talking and makes the decisions. The latter is a dialogue with the horse and rider relying on their education and experience.

If the horse is wrongly presented at a fence or if he meets it badly then very often this is going to be the cause of him stopping at it. Many educated horses, or horses with a strong instinctive sense of survival, will correct themselves and still jump the fence. Others, less

Here you can see the horse correcting and judging his own stride (as this is a very young horse undergoing basic training, I am using poles on the ground, but the principle is the same as cavalletti).

The horse has now regulated his stride to the distance of the poles

experienced, will lose their nerve, go past the point of take-off and are thus left no choice but to stop or crash into the fence.

It is very difficult for a rider who is not getting daily practice to reach the stage where rhythm becomes instinctive, but there is a little routine which can help him on this. It will only take about half an hour, but does require a horse that has been 'taught' to jump and a rider who is capable of 'listening'.

First of all put up two small fences, one a plain bar (a cavalletti does the job perfectly); this will represent an upright fence. The other will be two parallel bars set apart (two cavalletti, for example), which will represent a spread fence. Place the two obstacles near each other; I find it more useful to put them side by side, but their siting is not all that important. So we have in miniature the foundation of all the obstacles we can invent—an upright and a spread.

We start off by getting the horse to canter very slowly around the two fences, gradually letting him relax more and more, with the rider leaving him completely alone, until we reach the stage where the horse is 'lobbing' along on a very loose rein with the rider sitting quietly and doing nothing. When this is achieved we then let the horse go in and pop over the two small jumps *completely on his own with the rider just holding the neck strap or a tuft of mane.* That is to say let the horse do all the 'talking'; the rider must do nothing but 'listen'. Working

31

Two youngsters teaching each other. I have told the rider to leave the horse completely alone.

all the time on circles and by using large circles and small ones, approaching the little obstacles from different angles, sometimes coming in short or from a long way off and jumping the bars from both directions.

The rider, by feeling what is going on underneath him (that's the listening part), will find that the horse will get himself into a set rhythm, and through this rhythm he will judge his fences; on occasions just accelerating slightly; on others steadying himself just before take-off. Then the horse will show the rider (that's the talking part) what happens when he meets one wrong; for instance, if he comes in at a very sharp angle he will put in one or several short strides to balance himself and then jump, or will put in one extra long stride and then jump. If he does not correct his stride when he is 'wrong' you will feel him almost stop and then lift himself into the air jumping too big over the bar or he will actually 'stop', deciding that discretion is the better part of valour. Further he will show you that he prefers to get close to the upright fence so that he can use the arc of his back to get the height, whereas he will take off further away at the spread fence in order to flatten his back to get the length. Whilst this is going on you will find, at first by instinct, later by judgement, that you will begin to take part in the conversation by seeing and feeling when your mount is coming in wrong. Automatically you will start pushing him with your seat bones when you see the long stride is needed or more impetus is called for, then you will start checking slightly with your hands as you see the short stride is needed. By working from long distances and short distances you will find that it is easier for the horse on the long approaches and you will learn to judge the moment when to interfere with him and when to leave him alone. On the shorter approaches your mind will react quicker as will the horse's body.

That's how to see those magical strides, and to take advantage of the 'conversation'. Now study the diagrams that attempt to illustrate this delicate (and difficult) aspect of equitation. I have given only a few examples of the right way to ask your 'questions'. This is very much the responsibility of the rider; he must be honest with himself. For example, did you ask for that movement in a simple manner? Did you present the horse at the fence giving him every chance to understand and to jump it? Are you 'listening'? And are you really on talking terms or are you just passing friends?

If all fails and the horse continues to object then I repeat what I said earlier: get rid of him or stop jumping him. Neither of you gain anything from fighting each other every day.

Good position and feel

Normally when we speak of position we mean the technicalities of a good 'seat'—the position in the saddle, the placing of the legs and hands, the use of the seat bones. The mechanics of this I have already dealt with in *Progressive Steps in Riding*. Further, there are many good text books on the various seats and styles, their uses and their purposes. In this section I want to talk about the position behind the position and the feeling behind the feel.

There is no point, and unfortunately it is a mistake many amateurs make, in having the most perfect seat if it is not in unison with the horse and his cadence, or if he is stumbling and floundering about unbalanced.

When finished, don't forget—let him relax.

There is no point in closing the left hand and opening the right hand if the horse does not have an educated mouth. He will not have the faintest idea what you are talking about. These statements may sound rather cynical or contradictory but I can assure you they are not meant to be. You see we are discussing something beyond the A B C, and all that you have learnt from that A B C must now be adapted to the real core of the subject, that of working with a living creature. As with all living things, rules and regulations sometimes have to be bent a little.

Recently the wife of a friend of mine asked me if I would come and watch her practising for a rather important dressage test. Both my friend and his wife are excellent riders in the technical sense and they have some very good horses, though neither are what you might call 'lifetime' riders.

On arriving at the yard I was absolutely amazed to see one of the finest little private stable-yards I have ever seen in my life. Everything was impeccable, horses, boxes, saddlery; even the muck heap was tidy! This morning, I thought, I'm going to see something marvellous. We made our way to a full-size international dressage arena that had been specially laid down for practice. Madame P. entered and began her dressage test. She was a particularly intelligent person and very ambitious to make her mark in the world of dressage. She had asked me to advise her because, she, herself, could see nothing wrong but she was not getting into the winner's box.

I sat and watched with her husband, himself a well-known show-jumper, and immediately one could see what was happening—it lacked life—it lacked gaiety—there was no feel. Horse and rider were not on the same wavelength. They executed all the movements correctly but mechanically. I asked her to stop, and explained what I thought. She was trying to be too perfect; her aids were obvious; her position was classic but rigid. The horse was obeying but he was not interested. It is rather like me playing a tune on the piano (and I can). You will recognize the tune but give that same piece to Rubinstein and it will come alive. Now we are not all Rubinsteins or international dressage riders, but we can put life and gaiety into what we are doing. This is what sport is all about—fun.

To return to Madame P., she agreed and thought it was because she was over-practising. I suggested to her that instead of practising

Put feeling into it.

the movements in sequence, I should call out the movements out of sequence and for every one she did not do immediately it would cost her a beer each for me and her husband. She soon relaxed and we were all laughing. In addition, the horse was more gay; he was putting more impulsion and more energy into it. It was not the best of dressage tests, but my word it was *alive*, and I guarantee you that that young lady will be in the French dressage team before very long.

The moral is, of course, respect the rules, study the text books, have a good seat, keep a good position, but don't let your riding become rigid or too unnatural, and above all avoid letting your horse become jaded or stale. Through your 'feel' and your 'listening' keep it alive and flowing.

Feel what is going on underneath you and put *feeling* into it.

3 Relaxing the mouth and jaw

The most important step in 'conversation' is the establishing of communication between the horse's mouth (the bit) and the rider's hands
(the reins). It is here that most of us make our most basic mistake in
so far as we try short cuts rather than trusting to time and patience. A
horse with an uneducated mouth is practically useless, and certainly
inefficient; through his ignorance a sequence of events will be set up
causing all sorts of complicated problems. Furthermore the animal will
be a difficult and uncomfortable ride. Now as I have said before, some
people like difficult rides. I do not; and what is more, although I have
never heard one say so, neither does the horse. One generally finds that
badly ridden and poorly trained horses are bad eaters ('bad doers' is the
term'), worriers in the loose-box and never look healthy or well con-
ditioned.

The object of relaxing the mouth and jaw is not only for communication but also to encourage the horse to carry his head in the most
natural and comfortable position whilst carrying a rider, rather like a
simple lesson in deportment. If a mannequin carries her head badly,
too high or too low, it will affect the movements of her whole body.
A mannequin who moves badly will soon be under-employed. Equally
if the horse is allowed or made to carry his head too low or too high he
too will move badly and the rider will have problems in employing him
to the full.

So much for the object, but why do we ask the horse to relax the
jaw? There isn't really an answer to this question; it is more a 'choice'.
When the horse is in his natural state, say in a field grazing, he has two
ways of using his body when he wants to move. He can lengthen it for

38

Horse 'overbent'.

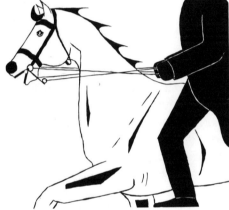

Raising his head.

Good position—accepting
bit.

long strides and he can shorten it for short strides. If a young horse is in a paddock on his own and we turn out another young horse with him, the two of them will raise their heads and arch their necks (bringing their bodies into a shortened form), they will look at each other for a few seconds, then suddenly turn and shoot off around the field, but this time lowering and extending their heads and necks (bringing the body into the lengthened form). In other words when the horse wishes to contain the energy and activity of his body, by using his head and neck, he makes himself shorter. When he wishes to release that energy, again by using the head and neck, he can make himself longer. It is safe to assume the horse knows the best way to use his own body; so we must educate him to 'cash in' on this natural technique whilst being ridden and controlled by us. This is not quite the same thing as running around a field with nobody on his back. In order to do this we have invented 'tack' to put on him.

The saddle was thought of mainly for our comfort. The bridle was the first item to be thought of, because it is here that we have the greatest control over the animal's body. Quite simply the bit operates on the tongue, the lips, and the bars of the mouth (bars being the upper part of the lower jaw). Some bits work on the roof of the mouth as well but that need not concern us here. Now if we are going to communicate with the animal through putting a lump of steel into what is an extremely sensitive part of his body, then we must do it in such a way that he understands without discomfort. So we work to get the horse to accept the bit in his mouth as naturally as possible, then we can take advantage of his natural ability for collection (the shortened form) and for extension (the lengthened form). In order to have the horse and his paces at our beck and call, as it were, we must have his front end light and his back end active. In the simplest form, this is collection. It is from this point on that the 'choice' comes. There are two ways open to us to attain this shortening and extending. We can urge the horse forward thus encouraging the hindquarters to be active whilst we restrict the speed of the forward movement by the pulling action of our arms and hands. This can be effective, but the horse can only support, not just resist but support, the pulling action by stiffening his jaw and thus setting his body against this force. The only way he can offset the pressure on the bars of his mouth is by putting force against it in a biting action. The alternative is to educate the horse to a signal from which he will accept the bit and relax his jaw, thus making life easier for himself and the rider and furthermore ensuring that he uses himself in a more natural manner.

This is something which you can see for yourself and something the horse will show you (conversation?). Watch a horse working on the lunge-rein, with his saddle and bridle on, but with the reins loosely placed over the pommel of the saddle and under the stirrup leathers. If the animal is allowed to relax thoroughly and just saunter around at a slow walk, he will tend to carry the head low and eventually make contact with the bit himself. At first he will 'play' with the bit, stiffening and relaxing his jaw, but finally closing his mouth and continuing to walk around unperturbed. When asked to collect himself and to trot he will immediately raise his head. Note though, that this time he will keep the mouth closed and the jaw relaxed.

This is the case with a horse that has had a correct basic training. With a horse that has been given insufficient elementary education the opposite is the case—he stiffens the jaw. This type will do this in all his paces, showing you the standard of his training (conversation?).

Returning to the animal, we are watching one that is beautifully schooled and impeccably educated . . . of course. The interesting thing here is that the horse will nearly always show his collected paces, especially at the trot and canter, raising his head slightly for each gait, and rounding his neck. By doing this he is containing his energy and

The young horse not accepting her bit. Now she has accepted it.

engaging his hindquarters whilst remaining relaxed in his mouth and jaw. Conversely, if asked to extend any of these paces, the walk, trot or canter, the horse will lower his head and extend the neck thus releasing the contained power of his hind-legs to propel him further forward. As I have said in my earlier books, with the horse the engine is in the back. In the extensions he must remain relaxed in the jaw.

Here, once more, you have witnessed the horse's part of a dialogue. The horse has shown you which is the best position of his head (for him) and has explained to you how much he knows. Now comes the difficult part: you must now turn this into a direct conversation between the two of you. One would have thought that the next logical step would be to get onto the animal's back and try to achieve the same results as one has seen from the ground. This can, most certainly, be done. But I think in order to take the 'conversation' onto a slightly higher plane it is better to go through just one more exercise. From this we should be able to get the 'talk' flowing: it's far better to feel our way in the dialogue and not to force our way through it.

A pair of elastic reins will be needed for this and a drop-noseband, preferably a lightweight one, and a horse that is not completely nuts.

The drop-noseband must be fitted carefully, not too tightly, and must only be used with a simple snaffle bit.

The elastic reins will have lengths of elastic about six inches long. This elastic must not be too weak or too strong, the former being better than the latter. It must 'give' to any movement of the horse's

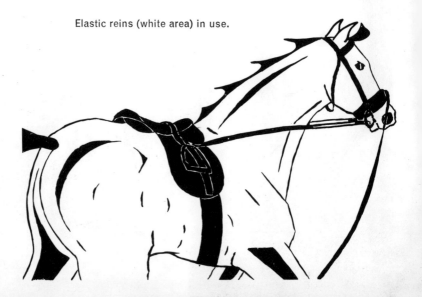

Elastic reins (white area) in use.

head but not just to the weight of his head. The reins will be fitted to the bit and, as before, pass under the leathers and over the pommel. The difference this time is that these reins are shorter than the normal. They must not on any condition be tight or taut, as this will only teach the horse to stiffen his jaw, then his body and finally his action. The elastic reins should be fitted in such a way that there is a contact with the mouth when the horse is walking.

The drop-noseband which passes under the jaw and outside the bit will encourage the animal to concentrate on the bit and the reins. It will not make the horse relax its jaw.

Once more, study the horse whilst he is working on the lunge, starting with the walk and going through the transitions to the canter. The elastic reins will encourage the horse to continue the natural changes of his head carriage, as we have seen earlier, whilst simulating the control of the rider's hands on his pace. This time, though, you will not only be 'listening' by looking but you will be starting to 'feel' what is required when you finally ride the horse.

At the beginning of the exercise the animal will tend to play with the bit more than he did before, but given time to find his balance he will relax and take the contact of the bit. The give and take of the elastic reins will allow him to find the most comfortable carriage; having discovered it, he will keep it.

You have seen it. The horse has seen it. Now comes the big moment, get on him and ask the same 'question.'

Begin by allowing the horse to relax thoroughly on a loose rein. Let him stretch and blow his nose. Then gather up the reins and make him stand, take up the contact with the mouth and ask him to walk

Drop-noseband correctly fitted.

Giving his mouth.

forward whilst with the hands closed and low not allowing him to. At first he will stiffen the jaw against your closed hands. Keep asking the same 'question', then (quite suddenly you will find) he will raise his head slightly, tuck it in and you will feel him relax the jaw thus keeping a light contact with you and walking forward. Let him walk on and then repeat the process again. You have said 'relax your jaw' and the horse has replied by giving his mouth to you. The contact between the horse's mouth and the rider's hands is the most important and basic facet of the conversation between the beast and the man. If there is a golden rule or magic formula then perhaps this is it—the education of the horse's mouth and the rider's hands.

Continue at the walk, keeping the contact and the horse's mouth relaxed. Should you lose the contact or should the horse stiffen his jaw against you make him stand, and ask the question again.

What has in fact happened is that the horse has learnt a vital system of communication with your hands from which he will gain comfort. Eventually with the mere squeezing (closing) of your hand the horse will give his mouth. You have learnt a subtle and very advanced practice of equitation.

You see the horse will relate the closing of your hands, when you restricted his forward movement, to the relaxing of his mouth. On the other hand you have started talking to him by the simple signals of opening and closing your hands—a secret and almost unseen dialogue and so much more easy than pulling (for both of you!).

This conversation by feel can now be expanded to the other paces. Work on medium-size circles in both directions. Remember from your earlier instruction that the horse's body must bend to his circle and that his head must point in the direction of the circle. Therefore we must make the conversation a little more sophisticated. The conversation will take place between the inside hand (the right hand if riding to the right) and the horse's mouth. Contact with the outside hand must not be lost but kept very light. By closing and opening (in a squeezing action) the horse will recognise the 'phrase 'and give his jaw (relax it), bringing his head into a natural position. Once the conversation is really flowing between you and all feels good—you and the horse are both relaxed and comfortable—start enlarging the circles until eventually including some small jumps. Bring in changes of direction by moving directly

44

from a circle to the left to one to the right. In the former the rider is talking with his left hand and the horse with the left side of his mouth. In the latter the rider is talking with his right hand and the horse with the right side of his mouth.

Each time the dialogue breaks down, go back to square one and start again.

This phase in the rider's (and the horse's) education is the hardest, the longest and the most important. Until the rider can start, continue and finish the conversation of the 'hands' and 'mouth' he cannot become an accomplished horseman.

Giving the poll

This is in fact almost the same thing as the giving of the jaw. In general a horse that stiffens his jaw also stiffens his poll.

I kept this separate because there are just a few points I wish to make. The rider must concentrate on the horse remaining relaxed all the time. He must go through with his conversation. A horse that is not relaxed or does not understand, or quite simply is trying to avoid the job, can, by raising his head higher than normal and by stiffening his poll avoid contact with the bit. In other words the dialogue of the hands and mouth can be stopped there and then. Should this happen then the solution is as before: stop the conversation and start again.

The stiffening of the neck will stiffen the back, shorten the action of the legs, and the result is the loss of impulsion.

When the horse says 'yes'

If we have the intelligence and the training to permit the horse to go about his work with the minimum interference from us then the horse will say 'Okay, let's go.' Equally if the horse has the education and training to give us an easy comfortable ride, we will say 'Okay, let's go.'

To achieve this happy state of affairs we must have the patience to wait for the horse to say 'yes'. You are the one who is asking the questions, not him—simple, isn't it?

Not much you might say, to warrant a separate item in such a technical chapter, but better by far than getting lost in my or anyone else's pontifications—keep it simple. Think about it.

45

Large honest ears.　　　Small 'piggy' ears.　　　Lop-eared.

4 The language of ears and body

You know the many old sayings that people have, like: 'You can tell he's dishonest, look at those shifty eyes', or 'A man with a beard has something to hide'. Fortunately there is very little truth behind this and even less science. I have a very good friend, though, who can determine a child's future or a man's character by the shape of his ears. Yes, really, and much as I hate to admit it, he is often right. For instance, he says that those who have ears that stick out are likely to be very musical, singers or dancers, and that people with small ears have criminal tendencies!

As to the possibilities of this being accurate with human beings, I would not know, but with horses in general this could be true up to a point.

The old horse-dealers in the not so distant past had many ideas on the subject (the operative word here being 'old'). The real horse-dealer was a man who placed his horses. The horse-dealers of today are men who sell horses and ponies, and what rubbish many of them sell too. If a poor unfortunate creature is capable of launching himself at least three feet into the air 'they' will guarantee him as a great show-jumper. The fact that the equally poor unfortunate creature that is going to attempt to ride such an animal may break his neck in the process, does not come into it, of course.

The real horse-dealer, the old professional, was a great judge of the horse; he bought his horses for selling to a particular rider. It is from them that we have inherited some of our sayings—our yard-sticks if you like. For instance, a horse with long wide ears is normally an honest, generous horse. One with small, pointed, wide ears, a difficult personality, often dishonest. An animal with small 'piggy' ears, a downright villain;

46

watch him. A horse with floppy ears (flop-eared or cow-eared) is often a placid, rather sleepy type but a great stayer, with plenty of stamina. Once more one cannot say that this information is backed by science and it is purely general. Although there are many other factors to be considered when judging a horse, I have found some of these old sayings very helpful.

Do not forget, as I have said earlier, there are no hard and fast rules and in the end 'handsome is as handsome does'.

The language of the ears

Now, old wives' tales many of the sayings may be, but there is a certain element of truth in them: the horse's ears are important. Apart from the fact that without them he would be stone deaf, he also 'talks' with them. That is to say that if the rider is perceptive to them, there are certain signs given by the ears that can be 'read'. We have discussed before the necessity to warm the horse up before he and the rider start work. This is done to attain a relaxed mental attitude and a supple body. A relaxed horse will tend to let his ears flop almost in rhythm with his movement. The ears will droop slightly and the animal is thinking of nothing in particular; he has no mental distractions, he has accepted his bit and is ready and waiting for instructions. You must be careful here to distinguish between a lop-eared animal and a tired horse, as drooping ears are commonly a sign of tiredness. They can be a sign of fatigue or illness (usually only in the box). Again I think it can be left to your intelligence to know the difference between a relaxed horse and one that is dying on his feet from weariness.

When the horse is concentrating, in other words when he is with you and his mind is on his work, he will hold his ears stiff, more erect, some-times cocked forward, sometimes turning one or other backwards. He is attentive to you, attentive to what is happening in front of him, listening to (watching, in a way) all that surrounds him.

One ear *turned* forward, one *turned* backwards.　　Ears *turned* back.　　Ears *pinned* back.

The perplexed, confused horse that simply does not understand will tend to turn his ears back, then forward, and back. In this case it is extremely difficult to generalise but the important thing here I want you to note is that he turns the ears. He is trying to pick up some sort of message. A horse in new surroundings for the first time, a new loose-box or a change of paddock, will tend to make the same signals. Give him time to settle down or to orientate himself. He will sort out for himself what you want of him or where he is—if you give him time. Do not force your will on a confused horse, just keep quietly and calmly repeating the question in its simplest form. Let him get it into his little brain himself then you will find it will stay there for life.

The real bad character, the 'villain' as we call him, will lay his ears flat back on the top of his neck. An attacking horse will do the same. The difference here is that he lays the ears back not simply turning them. There is no need to avoid the fact that this sort of horse does exist, but in my experience the *majority* are man-made. These creatures have usually been badly handled or poorly trained and in some cases over-training has turned them sour.

The horse, then, basically uses his ears to listen with, but if the rider is paying attention, there are signals to be read. We are now beginning to get some sort of structure to our riding dialogue, another aspect of the secret 'conversation.'

The language of the body

Here there is a parallel with the old sayings, such as 'Watch a redhead, she will have a terrible temper', 'A man with a high forehead is intelligent', etc. The old dealers had their own rules of thumb. They did not like a horse with a 'bump', an enlarged forehead between his eyes—a dishonest one, they would say. They did not like a horse with four white socks— no courage; or a chestnut horse—always too hot (excitable). There is no doubt that there is some truth in these points.

We have discussed the shape of the horse but over and above this the animal does give us certain signals with his body. If you, the rider, are not relaxed it will transmit to the horse and he will find it difficult to relax. At the same time if you are confident and clear in your instructions to

48

Start off your warming up quietly and calmly.

him, this, also, will transmit. But what happens when the transmissions operate in the other direction, from horse to rider?

One of the best ways this can be illustrated is by making a short study of the 'warming up' process. We all, man and beast, need some sort of warming or loosening up before making any physical or mental effort. I know I do; it takes at least four cups of tea in the morning before I can even start thinking, let alone actually moving.

Too often one finds that riders tend to think that getting a horse ready for work is a question of either getting him very excited and keyed up or getting themselves excited and keyed up. It is probably more the latter; perhaps they need to before tackling the job in hand. With some the object seems to be to tire the poor animal out. Unfortunately one sees far too much of this, particularly in show-jumping.

The whole point in warming the horse up is to get his body supple and his mind relaxed. If the exercise is carried out correctly then the rider will also be supple and relaxed.

Each horse differs immensely as to how much limbering up he needs.

49

Some need only fifteen to twenty minutes, others as much as an hour. This will depend upon his temperament (and very often his breeding) and the weather. A thoroughbred horse will take less warming up than a non-thoroughbred, is warmer blooded and will be more affected by the weather and conditions around him. A mountain pony will be less influenced by a high wind than say a pony from the lowlands and so on.

As you know from what has been discussed earlier, we start off by letting the horse walk around the yard or the paddock on a loose rein, exactly as he pleases. To begin with, his movements will be quick and rather jerky, he will look around him, he will be listening, moving his ears. In other words his body is saying, 'I've only just pulled out of the box, let's see what sort of a day it is. Give me a few minutes to feel my feet.' We all do this first thing in the morning, so why not an animal?

The time of the day must be taken into consideration here and also the weather. Early in the morning one gives the horse a little longer than after lunch. If the weather is cold, windy, or it's raining, the horse will take longer to settle. Should there be a particularly high wind it will take considerably more time before he can concentrate. Nothing is more difficult than being asked to concentrate when there is a strong wind blowing. Then again, in very warm weather the animal will relax much more quickly.

Start off slowly with the exercise of asking the horse to give his mouth, to relax his jaw. Gradually as the horse warms up his movements will become smoother and more flowing. The rider will know this because he will feel more comfortable in the saddle. There are two very important signals or statements that the body makes at this moment. They are very simple and natural, and I have yet to see a horse or pony that does not do it. First, as the horse relaxes he tends to breathe regularly and in rhythm with his movements. Sometimes one can even hear the breath passing through the nostrils—at the trot with a two-beat sound and at the canter to a three-beat time. The second is that as the breathing becomes regular the horse will literally blow hard down his nose two or three times cleaning out his nostrils. This is the body saying, 'All right, I'm ready now, what are we going to do?' I have yet to 'read' these two signs and find that the horse was not limbered up and ready for business.

There is another aspect to the signs the horse's body will give you. So far we have talked about the signs to be read when the animal is not

50

physically ready to work, but what if the horse is not mentally ready? Normally the body and mind work hand in glove, certainly in the context we have discussed, of training and discipline. Yet a situation can arise when the body is relaxed but the mind is not receptive. There are two main causes of this, they are lack of education (of either rider or horse), or the failure of the horse to understand. As in so many cases of training based on routine there are common signs that show themselves more than others, and it is these I intend to use to explain this point.

One of the most powerful (as against important) aids we have in controlling and in giving signals to the horse is our leg. With the legs we control the 'revs of the engine', the impulsion, and through this control we can regulate the accuracy of what we are asking the horse to do. Here is where the value of this aid lies. It is an 'asking' aid and it operates on one of the most delicate areas of the animal's body, the rib-cage and girth, where the horse's skin is extremely thin. The rider's legs are not an instrument of punishment. Giving the horse a kick in the ribs with your heels may give you some satisfaction but it will not encourage the animal to respond to a fine leg aid, quite the opposite: it will make him 'leg shy', and he will move away from the leg, thus creating problems for the rider in keeping the horse's action smooth. Worse still, the horse will become frightened of the leg aid and this will only create confusion in his mind. Confusion, as you already know, must be avoided at all costs.

So before we can start working the horse with our legs, we must be sure he is ready to take a direct question—he must be fully warmed up, supple and responsive. Furthermore the horse and the rider must have reached a sufficient standard of education. Should the rider apply too strong a leg aid in the wrong position, say too far back, or before the horse is ready, then the horse will answer back directly. This brings us back to the common signs because the horse will give his negative response in one of two ways. One, he will kick out sideways at the offending aid, with what is called a 'cow-kick', or, two, he will swish his tail violently at the irritation.

This is yet another side to the conversation but this time there is a difference. The rider has asked a direct question either badly or at the wrong moment. As the French say, never talk business until the cheese course! The horse, by 'cow-kicking', has been able to give a direct answer, saying, 'Stop that, I don't like it!' The less aggressive animal will react by an energetic and quick swish of his tail to show his dissatisfaction, but he is still making the same negative reply. If the rider continues in this fashion then the conversation becomes an argument. In an argument of this kind, somebody has to win; consequently somebody's going to get hurt, and this is only a waste of time and energy for both parties, which is non-productive. A vicious circle is put into motion until both man and beast are watching each other like hawks and waiting for the next encounter. Not a very rewarding way of getting results and any such results will be short-lived.

It is better that the rider should look for another way of posing his question. Let the horse 'slop' around a bit until he is once again relaxed or sufficiently supple to accept the aid and respond to it. Then the conversation will be two-way and the dialogue will continue, both sides understanding it.

I must qualify all this by saying that the horse will gently swish his tail or slowly cow-kick at his flanks or tummy if something such as a fly irritates him. This is perfectly natural, but once again you must use your intelligence to know the difference between the natural action and when he is doing it to get rid of you.

Finally whilst on the subject of the leg aids and their application, many riders seem to think that spurs will improve the response from the horse. This is true provided they are used properly. Spurs must be pressed against the horse's sides with the squeeze of the rider's calf. They are not for digging into the animal's ribs, and above all *they are not for punishing him.* Wrongly used spurs will produce the sort of objections we have been talking about, cow-kicking and swishing the tail, in double quick time and with far more violence. Worse still they will produce an ugly sight and a sour animal. A sour horse, like a sour man, will never achieve lasting results.

The spurs should be 'pressed' against the horse.

5 Riding a dressage test

There was a time when dressage was looked upon with some considerable awe. It was thought to be some sort of mysterious black magic that could only be performed by a small group of high priests and priestesses. Happily, thanks to the pony clubs and the riding clubs, it is now known and understood by the riding public at large. To some degree it is also due to the increasing popularity of one-day, two-day and three-day eventing, in which the dressage test is an integral part. For it is here that the value of a dressage test can be measured and seen in useful units.

Dressage comes from a French word and it means training or drill, nothing more and nothing less. In other words, basic training and discipline. Not, I hasten to point out, Haute École or High School riding; that is still for the magicians and circuses.

Everything you do with the horse is dressage—training. The dressage test, at all levels, is the proof of how you have trained him—drill. The test is a direct appraisal of how you have schooled and educated your horse. That is to say it is the end-product of your riding—it is not an exercise to show how pretty you look on his back.

So we can summarise a great deal of what we have so far discussed by riding a dressage test together. I have expressly invented a very simple test, just for us, which demands only the basic movements, i.e. walk, trot, canter, and the transition to these, changes of direction and the halt. Nothing fancy—so simple that you won't find it in any of the many riding manuals. Further I have cancelled out the usual cross to C or canter at H, etc. This would only make it too woolly and complicated both for you and for me!

Here is our imaginary dressage test:

i. Enter ring at walk, halt and stand.
ii. Collected walk to barrier, turn left, sitting trot.
iii. Half-way down arena, circle.
iv. Continue at rising trot to opposite side of ring.
v. Cross centre at sitting trot, turn right.
vi. Half-way down arena, circle.
vii. At finish of circle, collected canter.
viii. Cross centre at sitting trot.
ix. Turn left and collected canter.
x. Bottom corner of arena, sitting trot.
xi. Turn into centre.
xii. Halt and stand.
xiii. Leave arena at relaxed walk.

We have studied the test, nothing difficult. The horse is warmed up, down on his bit and ready for business. Our number has been called, so, thinking aloud, here we go into the test.

An imaginary dressage test shown in three stages.

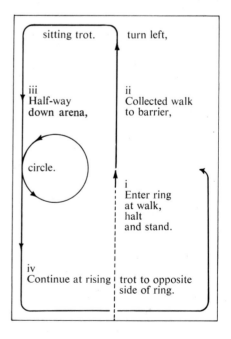

sitting trot.   turn left,

iii
Half-way
down arena,

ii
Collected walk
to barrier,

circle.

i
Enter ring
at walk,
halt
and stand.

iv
Continue at rising trot to opposite side of ring.

(i) *Enter ring at walk, halt and stand.* Several competitors have gone before us. They have all done the test, no end of people can, but ours is going to be different. Ours is going to be alive, gay, we'll show those judges what an easy lovely ride our horse is. They will wish it were themselves riding him. Like the man said in his book, nothing mechanical, listen to the horse. We have a good active walk, hands are in contact with the horse's mouth, his head position is relaxed. Now that halt and stand; must keep the horse's impulsion by the squeezing of our legs. We've come to a good halt, the horse's weight is equal on all four legs, his mouth is relaxed and closed, his ears are moving waiting for the next move.

(ii) *Collected walk to barrier, turn left, sitting trot.* That turn at the barrier to left, we must keep our horse's head pointed in the direction of turn without him raising it. It's best to imagine the turn like the beginning of a circle. Keep the left hand closed, relax slightly the right hand, especially the fingers. Try not to lift the left hand—those judges must not see our 'conversation'. Rather more pressure with the left leg than with right,

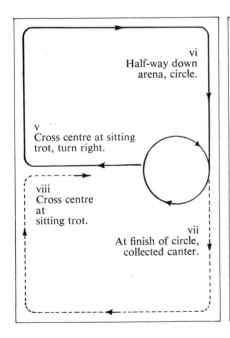

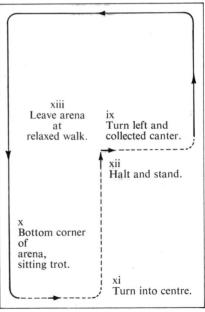

to encourage our horse to bend his body to the turn. Now get into that trot smoothly from the walk. No point in starting off like a performing kangaroo, therefore the leg aid must be light—close both legs to him—hands closed—made it. A slight swish of his tail: we may have been a little too heavy with leg aid. A long way to go at sitting trot now, so not only must we keep the impulsion but also the rhythm constant and even. Without this we are not going to be able to sit *into* the saddle and remain relaxed and still. There is no point in having our legs and head waving and flopping about like a conductor's baton.

(iii) *Half-way down arena.* We must wait until we arrive at exactly half-way down before starting the circle. There must be no anticipation either by ourselves or the horse. Anticipation will kill the smoothness and we want to show the jury that our horse is the most educated. Again pay attention to that circle, it must be round, not oval-shaped. Left hand closed, right hand more relaxed, use the inside leg as a pole for the horses body to bend around, the seat and legs keeping the activity. We must not forget the performance must be *alive*. Return to the original line; our horse must be kept on a single track, hindquarters following directly the line of the forehand. 'Feel' all the time what is happening, 'listen' to his body.

(iv) and (v) *Continue at rising trot to opposite side of ring and cross at centre at sitting trot, turn right.* Here we have got to be careful because at the rising trot it is more difficult to keep our horse's activity, or to put it another way it is going to be very easy to lose the impulsion and the flow. This we can counteract by 'squeezing up' our horse with both legs when we come down into the saddle. Regulation of this will depend on what sort of 'feel' our horse is giving us. Too much impulsion will make our horse 'heavy' in our hands and give the impression that he is over-bending (over-arching his neck). Cross the arena at sitting trot. We must sit down into the saddle, no flopping about. Turn right, so on changing direction, right hand and legs will be active.

(vi) and (vii) *Half-way down circle to right. At finish of circle, collected canter.* No problems here, same as previous circle though our aids will be the opposite way around. Here comes the clever bit: at the finish of this circle we must go into a collected canter. As before, no anticipation, the transition must be smooth, but as we are cantering to the right the off-foreleg must lead. So the pressure of the left leg must be stronger than the right and slightly further back, hands closed and still. Our horse's head must continue to point in the direction of the track. We have made the transition but our horse's head came up a bit too high: we must have been a little too 'fixed' with the hands. He seems to have settled again and the 'feel' is good. The cadence of the canter is important here—his head must be relatively still, and our body movements must not be over-emphasised.

(viii) and (ix) *Cross centre at sitting trot. Turn left and collected canter.* The transition up to the canter is easier to 'feel' because we are simply asking the horse to increase his pace. Therefore keeping his impulsion with our legs and seat is within the sequence of the movement. Rather like driving a car, it is easier to change up the gearbox without the car jerking than it is to change down. When changing to a lower gear with a car one listens to the engine to judge the right moment to make a smooth change.

Our collected canter is going well but on turning to cross the centre we must go back to the sitting trot. Remember that we want smoothness in our performance and that this transition is going to be important and closely watched by the judges. What are we going to do? Ask for the transition just before the turn or after? It would be too risky to ask for it on the turn; we may upset the balance of the test. No, the collected canter is good so we will ask for the trot before the turn, thus making it less complicated to keep our horse on a straight track. So we must feel and listen to the engine (at the back don't forget!) for the right moment. If we can 'ask' our horse at the moment the hind-legs begin to come under him to give the drive to his next stride, he should be able to make the 'change down' smoothly. The power of the hind-legs to propel can also be used, as with the engine, as a braking force. We are coming up to the turn, the moment is right. With both legs, squeeze the horse up to our firmly closed hands, not forgetting that with the push of our seat bones we can keep the impulsion right through the transition.

We have got to keep in mind that these transitions are perhaps the most important proof of the standard of our horse's education. By their fluency and non-loss of activity they show his understanding and reading of the bridle and the aids. Further they demonstrate that we, the rider, and our horse are 'conversing' all the time—working as a team.

Sitting trot across the arena, then at the turn left ask for the canter. This time we want the near-fore leading. The left hand is closed, directing the turn, the right hand slightly open, stronger pressure with our right leg to encourage our horse to strike-off with the near-fore leading. Once again the judges will be looking for fluency, so we must be particularly careful not to be tempted to force the horse onto his leading leg with the weight of our body as this will look clumsy and exaggerated. Keep the canter even and gay.

(x), (xi) and (xii) *Bottom corner of arena, sitting trot. Turn into centre. Halt and stand.* Once more, concentrate everything we have on that transition. Imagine the 'gear-box' and feel all the time the movement and power of the 'engine'. Down to the sitting trot—we are nearly finished but must not anticipate the finish—and that sitting trot up to the centre must be straight. We must come to the halt and stand without losing our horse's impulsion. This is the last impression the judges are going to get of our performance, so let's make sure it's a good one. Coming up to the halt now, close our legs to the sides of the horse, don't let them move backwards or forwards; close our fingers to block the forward movement; push our seat-bones deep down into the saddle. All of which we have done simultaneously and our horse has come to a good halt, standing squarely on all four legs.

(xiii) *Leave arena at relaxed walk.* We can relax our hands now, letting the horse stand for a few seconds, then gently and with a long, loose rein we let him walk out of the arena, stretching his neck, relaxing and knowing that his end-of-term exams are finished.

Well, there we are, you have ridden a dressage test without leaving your armchair! Fun, isn't it? I hasten to point out that this test was a pure figment of my imagination and not indicative of the average test, but I hope our dream journey has helped you to understand the workings of the 'conversation' between horse and rider.

Now, as in all fantasies, no problems presented themselves and no faults were committed, so what about the problems that can arise, and the most common faults that we see in reality?

Again—afterwards, let her relax.

The rider thinking of himself

Many riders seem to think that a dressage text is an exhibition of their riding when in fact it is the opposite—it is an exhibition of what a good 'ride' the horse is. If we allow ourselves to adopt the mental attitude that it is the rider who is on show then the performance will become dull, will lack rhythm and smoothness in the movements, for the logical reason that the rider will be over-concentrating on himself and not listening to his horse. Consequently the horse will not bother to listen to the rider.

Perhaps the most common mistake made here is the rider who exaggerates or over-emphasises the movements of his own body. This one sees more in the canter and the transition to and from the canter. The overall impression is that the rider seems to be working ten times harder than the horse. One sees this too much even at international competition level. A good example of this, as mentioned, is the transition to the canter when asking for a leading leg. You will remember we did make a mental note of this whilst doing our little test, movement (ix). What often happens (and in fact for some it is an accepted school of thought) is that the rider, by moving his weight to one side and increasing the force of his 'seat', pushes the horse on to the leading leg. For instance, if one is asking for the near-fore to lead, one changes one's weight in the saddle to the left and pushes with the seat to the left thus forcing the horse to support this displacement of weight he is carrying by leading off with the left side of his body. The dangers here are, I think, pretty obvious. The first is that the rider moves in the saddle, there is a displacement of weight, and the horse will tend to change his cadence in order to correct his balance and to counteract the weight change. With the movement of these forces, (a) the rider's and (b) the horse's, extra movements will be created and therefore the fluency will be lost, resulting in a further loss of smoothness of execution of the transition and therefore picking up unwanted penalty points. The second danger is that the exaggerated action of the rider will make the 'conversation' obvious to the spectator, will present a picture of clumsiness, and will show, in an obvious manner, that your horse is not educated but dominated.

This system can be used as a back-up to the leg-aid when schooling a young horse, but once he has read the dialogue of the leg-aid it should be dispensed with. To appear in a public competition, no matter how small, and ride in this manner is only to prove to the jury that you have not done your homework.

One last hint here on the subject of transitions: do not under any circumstances look down. Any movement by the rider's head will result in an interaction with the rest of his body. Downward movement by the human head produces rounded shoulders and a 'round' back, but what is more important *vis-à-vis* equitation, the hands will move. In equitation, any unwarranted movement of the hands will affect the horse's mouth; consequently the horse's head will also move, and movement of the head produces movement of the neck. The neck, as we have discussed, is the animal's balancing pole, so the horse will be forced to correct his balance, and, what is worse, the dialogue between the rider's hands and the horse's mouth will break down.

Mechanical riding—dragging of the horse's feet

In all sports the basic idea is very simple; in football it is not difficult, you just kick a ball; in cricket it's equally simple, you just hit a ball; in riding basically it's simple you just sit on a horse. But is it that basic? Human nature being what it is we like to do things better than others and to the maximum of our capabilities. So it is with equitation:

any fool can make a horse go round in a circle but getting him to do that for you better than anyone else is what the sport is all about. If it becomes mechanical the animal will become bored and if he is bored you too will have the same reactions; sum total—no pleasure for anybody.

One obvious sign of this is the horse that drags his feet as if they were just objects on the ends of his legs and which he has to carry around with him. Now you and I know that this can be a sign that he is tired, but if we are reading the 'conversation' correctly it will be obvious if he is, in fact, tired. Very often it is the opposite that is happening, it is the rider who is too passive. Keep uppermost in your mind: Am I getting the best out of the animal? Is he 'listening' to me? Is he comfortable and going well? In other words forget about yourself and concentrate on the performance your partner is giving. That way you will get pleasure and enjoyment from your hobby.

Memo for the dialogue

As much as I hate bringing riding down to formulae and secret recipes, it is possible to sum up the ground we have covered in two simple statements.
   (*a*) Simplicity = smoothness = fluency = activity = good performance.
   (*b*) Under-activity = loss of smoothness = loss of fluency = poor performance.
These two are about the best guide-lines you can carry around with you whenever you ride. Whatever you do avoid complication and confusion.

Practice and the practice ground

Sport is not something that one can do at spasmodic intervals. Riding is no different in this respect, it is a physical exercise both for you and for your horse. It is better to practise half an hour a day than to practise two hours per week on one day only. A little practice every day will keep the muscles supple and they will stay supple. The suppleness of your body and the horse's is the whole foundation for getting

61

results, thus by practising regularly each day the results should be better and easier.

For those who compete or are preparing for competitions this is even more important. Practise every day, it does not matter for how long as long as it is every day and if possible at the same time each day. This way your horse will settle into a daily routine and will know what is expected of him. Racehorses, for example, are ridden out at the same time every day, early in the morning. This is the basis of good training. Nothing is more tranquil or peaceful than a racing-yard in the afternoon with the horses quietly munching away or lying down, knowing that nobody is going to bother them until the following morning.

Finally, do make sure that your practice or training ground is flat and in good condition. There is no point in asking your horse to carry out movements of a dressage test if the practice ground is a quagmire of mud. Equally one will not get great results if the ground is rock-hard, causing the horse to jar all his body each time he lands over a fence. If possible keep moving your practice ring or jumps around so that there is always plenty of grass cover.

If the conditions under foot are bad or uneven the horse will be concentrating all his mental energy on keeping himself going and he will not be listening to you. If this happens there will be no 'dialogue' between the two of you and if that happens, and I am sorry to be so brutal, it would be far better for both to go home and forget it!

Thinking of the weather

I have in fact touched on this aspect earlier, so I do not intend to dwell on it too much here but it is relevant.

If you arrive at the show ground all ready to compete and it is blowing a force nine . . . well, there isn't much you can do about it. Either you decide to go ahead and face it or you retire gracefully and fight again another day. Usually one chooses the former and makes the best of it. For training purposes, though, we do have more control over the conditions we work under. Most horses find it difficult to concentrate or to feel on form in a gusty cold wind or in driving rain, indeed it's equally difficult for human beings. Far better to rug the horse up well and give him a quick walk in the woods or on the downs. Should you be one of those fortunate people who have an indoor school then that's the solution and the best place to be in bad weather.

It may seem terribly 'outdoor' to brave the elements but I find the results very often do not justify the effort.

Don't forget—the engine's in the back!

'I can't stand badly made horses.'

6   A tale of two horses

We glibly talk of the horse's personality; I say glibly because those who
are not involved with horses seem to enjoy the old joke that all horsey
types tend to look like horses or adopt their horse's personality. Well, all
right, let everybody enjoy their fun because the human being, peculiar
creature that he is, likes to put his fellow men into pigeon-holes: the
horsey type, the doggy type, the boating, motoring, freedom-loving,
rose-growing type, and so on. Why not? It's fun and we enjoy ourselves and that's our privilege, but, to revert to my opening phrases,
in fact the opposite is true. The horse is a herdic creature, a follower,
and he tends to forfeit his personality for ours. A timid man will tend
to have a timid horse; a dashing type will tend to have a dashing type
of horse; a calm, cool type will tend to produce a calm animal. Why
this is nobody knows, but we do seem to be able to instill into the
animal our own character.

I remember once going along on a buying trip with a friend of mine,
a bloodstock agent. Our brief was to buy hunters that were good rides,
good jumpers and capable of bearing the weight of under-exercised
businessmen looking for good weekend sport. The word had obviously
got around the dealers, by the jungle-drums, that we were coming. All
sorts of creatures were pulled out for us to try: good, bad, and in-
different, the only constant thing about them all was the 'derby winner'
prices.

My friend and I took it in turns trying the various animals. At one
yard my companion climbed aboard a rather wiry looking little horse
that had been beautifully trained at carrying his head very high with
his mouth wide open! Something which the poor unfortunate beast

seemed to do with the maximum efficiency and discomfort, much to his handler's satisfaction! 'Go and try him over some fences', said the seller. And away went the two of them, out of the yard and over the fields. We waited and waited, minutes went past, then almost an hour. Finally, a very mud-spattered, dishevelled 'friend' walked into the yard carrying a bridle.

'Well, what did you think of him?', I said weakly, not knowing really what to say.

'Oh, he's not too bad,' came the reply, 'his only problem is that he has big ambitions but no way of carrying them out!'

That is in fact a true story. When dealing with animals (and for that matter human beings) it is vital to keep a sense of humour. Very often one does ride horses that have been made into 'bad rides', and likewise one often rides badly a horse that is a 'good ride'. Inevitably when these situations arise things can and do go wrong, so a sense of humour is imperative. Without it we would never be able to carry on and face the problems.

To illustrate further this point of making a study of your personality and the horse's character to create a conversation between you, let me relate an experience of mine some years ago.

I had at that time two well-known show-jumpers, one I shall call the big horse and the other the little horse.

The big horse was a really big horse. Not a heavy horse or clumsy creature but very tall, with a powerful body but narrow and fine. He was already a well-known international show-jumper with a very fine record but an inconsistent one. Further he had quite a reputation as a difficult horse to ride.

When he arrived I let him settle in for a couple of days, just walking out each day for a little bite of grass and some gentle lungeing. I then started to work in earnest to find out just how he and I were going to be able to operate together—looking for the point from which our dialogue could begin. This was an extremely fascinating period for me, because he was an animal that had already reached a certain age, was already fixed in his ways and attitudes. How, then, was I going to transfer my ways and my personality, which were completely opposite to those of the previous owner, on to what was in fact a relatively old horse. One thing was certain: I could not change my

66

style, so the horse would have to be re-educated and change his. My own theory was that if an animal such as this could produce certain results under difficult conditions then given easier conditions he must produce better results and more consistently.

Those first few days were the most important, and it was here that some very valuable clues presented themselves. Firstly, the big horse was kind and gentle in his box, ate everything that was given to him and was completely relaxed. Secondly, on the flat he was not a difficult ride and providing one sat still he seemed quite calm. But the moment one started schooling over fences, even very small ones, he became a power-house of nerves, excitement, and fear, launching himself in all directions at anything that came in his way. He would take off at some fences long before he got there, some he would be practically on top of the obstacle and then he would take off at the last minute. Others he would just crash through like some one-horse-muscle-powered tank. After such a session he would return to his box and refuse to eat until the following morning, no matter how tasty a morsel was placed before him .

One does not need a lot of brains to work out that this could not carry on. Riding the big horse at that time was like doing ten rounds with Muhammed Ali, and I'm no Joe Frazier! No, a system of re-education would have to be found. Before any conversation could be started between him and myself a study would have to be made of his personality and his history.

This is how I attacked it. I made a list of facts and guesses as follows:

Facts
(*a*) The big horse must have some jumping ability—his past record proved this. Inconsistent it may have been, but sufficient proof was there.
(*b*) The animal was by nature gentle and calm; this we know because in everything except jumping his manners were good.
(*c*) He was, under normal conditions, a good eater (good 'doer').
(*d*) The size or height of the obstacles did not worry him—again his record proved this.

Guesses
(*a*) He was used to being dominated completely, waiting, and indeed

relying, on the rider's physical control—in other words he could not or would not think for himself. This would have to be found out.

(b) His mind and body might have reached an age where re-education was too late; i.e. was he musclebound, etc.? If not, retraining was possible.

This then was the basis of the re-training programme. The history of the big horse spoke for itself and was fact; now the guesses had to be put to the test and turned into facts.

The first step was to school on the flat where we had no problems or worries; this would make it easier to get a dialogue going between us and encourage him to think for himself. For this I used a very simple snaffle-bit and a drop-noseband, asking him to give his mouth and to respond to the finer aids. At first he would get very fussed and frustrated. He didn't seem to know even the most simple of the rider's aids. If I closed my legs to him, up would come his huge head, and away we would disappear over the Surrey horizon; if I used the 'seat-aid' to keep his impulsion, the opposite would happen: he would over-bend his neck, his head would vanish somewhere between his knees and the result would be once more an unasked-for tour of the local hills. This situation, as you will appreciate, was becoming a bit of a nightmare and could not be allowed to continue. Not only because I, through sheer fright, was losing weight quicker than a jockey on a crash diet, but also because he, through not eating after each escapade, was beginning to look like a show-jumping hat-rack!

Next I tried carrying out our schooling sessions in the indoor school, following the principle that if the big horse was shut in he would not be able to run off anywhere. This worked, for he started to listen to me and to concentrate on what we were trying to do. At last a dialogue had been started and it continued and expanded. If you could have seen the fantastic transformation in this horse's personality you would have realised the tremendous importance we must give to the conversation between horse and rider. He started to put on weight, a lot of weight, he became more handsome, he even looked younger. He not only ate all his feeds but I also had to give him an extra one late at night otherwise he would knock the place down.

68

We were on our way at last. Now was the time for the big step—jumping.

I started him off in the elastic reins we were discussing earlier and on the lunge, mixing all the various jumps as much as possible. At first, as on the flat, he could not understand that he had a body and a brain to use and, more, that he was being given the freedom to use them. He was completely lost, not knowing how to measure his fences or to pace himself for the fences to come.

One important point here. When you are working a horse in this manner, especially a young one, do make sure that he is properly protected. You see, what in fact one is doing is to let the horse teach himself; that is to say the trainer is allowing the animal to get himself into 'trouble' *and* to get himself out of it. Naturally there will be occasions when the horse will knock fences down, so his joints must be protected by knee-pads, boots, or bandages on all four legs and by over-reach boots.

Some think that if a horse knocks himself on the bar of an obstacle he will be more careful next time. Well, that may be, but equally a 'knock' may frighten the animal and a frightened jumper will not have confidence. Jumping requires confidence and lots of it.

Because of the amount of work we had done on the flat, the big horse's adaptation to the new system was almost immediate. He quickly realised that his body was more supple, making the effort of jumping far smaller for him than he had been used to. Under saddle, the story was the same; our conversation was going well for us. He was an absolute joy to ride and to watch. His style was now fluent, accurate and calm, and he was not landing the other side of the fence with an earth-shattering thump any more. Further he was now eating like a horse!

Stupidly, I thought the job was done, but you see with animals we do tend to use human thinking when we should in fact be trying to understand how they think.

On the first reappearance in public he fell completely to pieces—it was a catastrophe. The old memories must have come rushing back into his mind, and once again he was launching himself at fences like a misguided missile. But at home he was becoming one of the best rides in the yard. Our dialogue was getting more fine, more accurate and more sensitive. So I decided to take one of the biggest gambles I have ever taken. In future, whenever he ran into trouble I would pull him up and politely leave the stage.

There were two risks in this calculation. First, had I got the patience and the nerve to carry this through? Remember that this was to be done in public, so a certain amount of nerve would be required—the study of the mentality of the rider that I keep talking about. Second, had he, the horse, the aptitude to benefit from this and, what is more important, had he the type of character that would not take advantage of such a situation, seeing it as a good way of avoiding work? This factor is the personality of the horse that I keep talking about.

It proved to be a traumatic year, full of disappointments and heartache, but the gamble paid off. The second season was what made it all worth while. The big horse and I were now on 'talking terms', not only at home but on the field of competition as well. He was now jumping clear rounds consistently. What a thrill it was to ride this immense horse over so many big show-jumping courses, pulling up afterwards as cool as if we had been for a quiet walk over the fields at home.

Alas, there is no great hero ending or happy-ever-after stuff. The big fella had a recurrence of an old unsoundness that had been a problem for a very long while, but this time it was beyond repair. It was an experience from which one learns more than could otherwise be learnt in a lifetime, and I will always be grateful to the big horse for what I know today.

We did not win any great fame or fortune, nor did we get in the record books, but, my goodness, did we enjoy ourselves, and what a fund of knowledge we gained!

The little horse was quite the other end of the personality spectrum. A small, well-muscled, beautifully made animal, with a bright and cheerful character. He had glamour, he knew it, and he certainly had no intention of hiding the fact. Whereas the big horse had done so much this fella had done very little. The small amount of education he did have had been well done, so here was every trainer's dream, the real no-complex, no-nerves McCoy. He had just begun jumping and as far as he was concerned it was all a bit of a game, not to be taken too seriously. It did not take very long, working on the lunge and under saddle, before he knew his job well enough to face the public test. The first time out in competition presented no problems either for him or for me; his enormous athletic ability and pride in himself was his greatest asset. Here was, if such a thing does exist, the perfect show-jumping horse. Apart from odd little troubles when meeting something too big or too complicated for him he never gave me a moment's worry. He is still relatively young so there is as yet no finishing line for the story, but I think you can see the point of my relating the two case histories to you in the context of this book.

These were examples of the analysis of the animal's personality and potential for the job we wish him to do. One could say, why do all this work to change the horse's ways, why not make the rider adapt to the horse? Well, this can be, and often is, done. We do have to change our style to a certain extent to suit each mount. All horses differ in some way from their fellows, but the basic techniques of equitation are, in fact, standard. Thus the rider who is forever changing his technique, as against his style, is in fact making life complicated for himself. With each change of technique must come a change in performance and from that a fluctuation in the margin of error. In all forms of sport, in order to be effective we must keep the margin of error constant and at a minimum. No, it is far better to educate the horse to standardise his technique with the rider's, and from this can come, whether the performance is good or moderate, only consistency.

Anne Moore on 'Psalm'.

7   Illustrated examples

This is a straightforward picture chapter with photographic examples I have chosen to show the finer points of riding being executed at the highest standard. I want you to study these and relate them, not only to the preceding chapters, but also to your own riding technique. Try to add your own comments and thoughts to those that I have given you with each photograph.

The above picture shows what I have been getting at. The horse has been given the freedom to use his muscular body, and, my word, isn't he doing it well! Notice the relaxed and closed mouth. The whole image is one of graceful power. The photograph to the right is an unusual angle, but this I have shown expressly so that you may study the horse's head. Look at those ears and the position of the horse's head. One cannot fail to see how relaxed and calm horse and rider

Gert Wiltfang on 'Askan', a winner at Wembley of the King George Cup.

H.R.H. Princess Anne, Badminton 1971.

are, when they are in fact jumping a very big fence. Above is a superb example of the horse knowing his job. Again, through studying the usage he has of his body, especially his head and neck, we can see that he is a creature who has a bit more than prep-school education. The horse's ears have it; that look of complete concentration because man and beast have no worries, and no worries equals one hundred per cent concentration. These two certainly aren't getting into a fluster over the job.

The popular belief in many circles is that the jockey is not an equestrian. This is mainly because he has to ride in a way that is completely different from other forms of equitation, with short leathers, etc. To be a top jockey it is not enough to be a good race-pilot, you have got to be quite an experienced horseman as well. Above you can see the jockey going down to the start with his mount collected. Compare this to the chasers in action (overleaf) and you can see that the jockey, as with other riders, must know what extending and shortening

is all about. Study the open and closed hand technique that can clearly be seen here. In all these pictures are examples of the 'gay and alive' quality I keep talking about. In fact I keep repeating myself on this so much that you must think it is some kind of hang-up. Well, it is! The horses look so active, and yet not strained, and the riders seem to be putting in the minimum physical effort. It is interesting here to note that the horses seem to have almost exactly the same head carriage, the

76

These principles apply not only to the sleek thoroughbred but to all horses, including those that work for their living. Look at the dark brown horse at the rear of this group flexing his neck and collecting himself.

same flexion, and their mouths are closed with no resistance against the bit or the rider's hands.

I always find it fascinating when looking at pictures like these that the horse, this strong and powerful creature, has become so much part of our everyday scene, what with racing, jumping, trekking, etc. Yet only forty-five million years ago he was no bigger than a dog!

Riding with a friend in Fontainbleau Forest.

8 Riding round the world

We have been discussing some quite delicate technical points and the riding dialogue between horse and rider. Now, like the horse in training, let's relax and have a look at the 'riding dialogue' of other nations.

As you will appreciate this is not really a ride round the world, which each day gets smaller but is still a very large place. It is but a whistle-stop tour of some of the leading riding countries of our planet.

France

France has a very long history of cavalry, and to this day the corner-stone of French equestrianism is the military. French riders tend to follow the school of thought that the horse must be well educated and then given as much freedom as possible by the rider, to carry out his job. This is not only practised in eventing and show-jumping, etc., but also in racing. In France the race-tracks are nearly all very flat and many are small and circular. The jockey's job is more to allow and encourage the horse to run fast rather than use tactics. All the training centres are centralised in the major towns, Paris, Lyons, Marseilles and so on, and the revenue from horse-racing betting is used for the betterment of equitation and horse breeding at all levels.

As yet, riding is not looked upon as a spectator sport of any impor-tance. The many very good international showjumpers are almost unknown to the public at large; even more so the leading event riders. In post-war years, as is the case in so many countries, weekend riding and riding holidays have become more and more popular. All riding schools (clubs hippiques or centres hippiques) are registered and all instructors must be qualified or be *bona fide* student teachers. Courses are open to all, amateur and professional, at the Military Academy of Saumur, and the national stud, the Haras du Pin.

The sport, except for horse racing, is controlled by three bodies. They are the Section Equestre Militaire; the Fédération Française des Sports Equestres (F.F.S.E.); and the Ministére de l'Agriculture; all horse activities are subsidised by the State P.M.U. racecourse tote betting system. There are now over 150,000 weekend riders at the ever-increasing number of equitation centres all over the country.

Germany

Along with Austria and Switzerland, Germany is the 'home' of classical dressage riding. The Germans are, perhaps, the leading exponents in the world of this form of equestrian competition. They like strong muscular horses and are very fortunate in having many native breeds that are ideally suited to this sport. As yet dressage competitions have not become what one might call a form of sporting entertainment, but show-jumping has a tremendous public following. There are many German riders known throughout the world of show-jumping for their skill and ability. Here again riding holidays are extremely popular and there are many well-organised centres where the most beautiful regions of this country can be seen from the back of a horse. The very first world driving championships were held at Münster in 1973.

Special training centres are operated on a regional basis for the training of riders, instructors and horses. The National Training Centre is based at Warendorf, where the National Olympic Games Committee has its headquarters.

There are some 300,000 horses in the Federal Republic of which only 2,000 are thoroughbreds and nearly 40,000 are registered with the breeding societies, the majority of these being original native breeds.

America

For us all, young and old, the home of the Cowboy and the Wild and Woolly West. Nevertheless this is one area where the horse is still

Josef Neckermann, the German gold medallist dressage rider.

looked upon as a working animal and his importance in the control
and surveillance of livestock is not underrated, the American quarter
horse being just about the most famous breed throughout the world
for this type of work. In horse racing the United States, with its highly

A rodeo horse in Grangeville, Idaho. The dialogue here is unprintable!

organised racetracks and training centres, has become a leading nation. The American thoroughbred can now be found in the blood-lines, and on the tracks, of many leading European countries. It is in show-jumping that America is perhaps one of the most interesting countries. This is one of the youngest nations in the modern world, and yet they have chosen as their national training policy of equestrian teams the Continental technique of working on the horse's co-opera-tion, and not on man's domination. They have updated, adapted and perfected it; they like good-looking thoroughbred horses for the job and they are not frightened to put in hours of work teaching their horses how to jump. There is no finer and more exciting sight than a leading American rider giving a display of quiet, easy, classical show-jumping. The consistently good performance of their national teams is proof of the wisdom of this policy.

Rodeos are still the second largest horse spectator sport. There are now over 6,000,000 horses in the U.S.A., largely due to the huge interest in horseracing and trotting-racing.

Italy

As Germany is the home of classical dressage riding, so Italy is the home and birthplace of the modern riding techniques we use today. It was men like Federico Caprilli and Piero Santini who revolutionised equitation with their then new-style 'forward seat'. Their teachings can be found in practically every riding manual, in all languages, and in civil and military academies.

Racing is, again, the number one horse sport with the public. Italian racecourses and stud farms are among the most beautiful in the world. The Italian thoroughbred can be seen regularly winning many im-portant handicaps and classic races throughout Europe, England and America. Although Italian show-jumping riders are very fine ex-ponents of the art of show-jumping, the sport as such does not have a great public following. The large, important shows, normally held on Sundays, do, obviously, attract large crowds. The leading riders in show-jumping and even more so in eventing, are mainly the military, riding foreign-bred horses. For show-jumping, English horses are particularly sought after. Riding holidays are extremely successful with tourists but weekend riding is not yet a national pastime. Italy has a relatively small horse population now with only some 2,000 stallions registered; two-thirds of these are of the 'working' horse breeds.

Spain

With the Arabian conquest of Spain in about the middle of the seventh century, the introduction of the Arab horse improved the blood lines of the native breeds. These fleet-footed, agile creatures are still used today by the Rejoneador. Señor Peraltas, one of the great Spanish equestrians and a master in the art of bullfighting on horseback, is world-famous for his dramatic dressage displays. The breeding of fine horses, especially the Andalusian, is something of which the Spanish are very proud.

Spain is *the* country for riding holidays. These are organised on a national level and are a very important part of the tourist industry. You can take your choice from the multi-starred luxury holiday riding strong Andalusian horses to the more straightforward pony trekking in the mountains.

Equitation is still very much under the influence of the once world-famous military schools. It is interesting to note that some 900 years ago the Spanish Charger, because of the eastern blood, was very much in demand. Indeed William the Conqueror rode one when he invaded England.

There are now about 500,000 horses in the country and the majority are of no specific breed; nearly fifty per cent are draught horses.

Russia

What is now called the U.S.S.R. may well be the region where the horse was first domesticated. The famous Mongolian Wild horse, a species which we believe dates back to the Ice Age, still exists and can be seen in Eastern Russia. The Soviet Union is, of course, a vast country and because of the considerable geophysical and geographical differences between the regions many native breeds have been established to suit local conditions.

Many think that Russia has a longer history of organised horse-

top   Russian troikas, which are raced every Spring at the Moscow Hippodrome.
bottom   Trotting: the final heat for the 'Peace' prize held in Russia.

breeding than any other country, and some forty-odd breeds are now recognised and registered.

With the general public, trotting racing is very popular, the most well-known stadiums being in Moscow, Odessa and Kharkov.

In recent years many Russian riders and horses have been seen competing in international eventing and racing. In fact they are now beginning to compete with some success in England and America and are being consistently placed.

Considerable State encouragement is given to the breeding of horses, mainly for agriculture and for export. Government inspectors visit regional stud farms and co-operatives to advise on the selection of stallions and on cross-breeding techniques.

Collective farm horsemen in competition during the 'cotton holiday' in Uzbekistan.

'Now it's *my* turn!'